Illuminated Spirit

THE WIT LECTURES
HARVARD UNIVERSITY
THE DIVINITY SCHOOL

Jean Vanier (1993) *From Brokenness to Community*

Illuminated Spirit

GOVINDAPPA VENKATASWAMY

The Wit Lectures
Harvard University
The Divinity School

PAULIST PRESS
New York and Mahwah, N.J.

Library of Congress Cataloging-in-Publication Data

Venkataswamy, Govindappa.
   Illuminated spirit: Wit lecture/by Govindappa
Venkataswamy.
      p.   cm.
   ISBN 0-8091-3462-4
   1. Spiritual life—Hinduism. I. Title.
BL1237.36.V46   1994
294.5'44—dc20   93-42476
                                          CIP

Published by Paulist Press
997 Macarthur Boulevard
Mahwah, New Jersey 07430

Printed and bound in the United States of America

FOREWORD

*H*is full name is Govindappa Venkataswamy, but we call him "Dr. V.," always with fondness.

I know Dr. V. through the Seva Foundation, where we are both board members, and where his singleness of purpose is legendary. Dr. V. lives to fight blindness, and whatever he encounters in life seems to sharpen his interest to the degree it might be bent to that purpose.

It is refreshing to see America through his eyes. When Dr. V. came to our first board meeting some fifteen years ago, it was one of his first trips to the States. Dr. Larry Brilliant, another board member, remembers Dr. V.'s keen interest in the utilitarian:

We had one of our board meetings at Camp Winnarainbow, a rustic kids' campground, where each of us bused our dishes after meals. Dr. V. was taken by the efficiency of the scrubber mounted on a hose that we would use to wash off our plates. You knew that six months later there would be a scrubber just like it in the kitchen at Aravind. I saw that with the very first computer I ever had, an old Osborne, which Dr. V. was fascinated by on a visit with us at the University of Michigan; within a year an Osborne

1

just like it was analyzing data at Aravind. The same with my first video camera; not too long after Dr. V. saw it, there was one being used at Aravind to make training tapes.

One of the images that impressed Dr. V. most on his visits to America was the Golden Arches of McDonald's. But through his eyes those arches took on a transcendent meaning and bespoke a higher possibility. Why, Dr. V. wanted to know, couldn't the assembly-line efficiency that made hamburgers available on the street corners of every town in America, at a price everyone could afford, be harnessed to the mission of fighting blindness?

And now, a decade or more later, the Aravind Eye Hospital that Dr. V. founded in Madurai, India, is arguably the most efficient eye-care institution in the world. It performs more eye surgery in a day than any other hospital anywhere, and every patient who pays for eye care subsidizes two who cannot. The quality of care ranks with the best; ophthalmology students from institutions like Harvard and Johns Hopkins regularly rotate through Aravind for training. Aravind is one of a dozen or so institutions designated as Centers of Excellence by the World Health Organization—a testament to Dr. V.'s singleness of purpose.

That singleness of will is evident, too, in the fact that Dr. V. has become a superb eye surgeon despite what is perhaps the most striking thing one notices on meeting him for the first time: his fingers are twisted and frozen by an arthritis that struck him while he was in medical school.

Another image I have of Dr. V. speaks to his remarkable ability to transcend this disability. I remember seeing Dr. V. early one morning sitting serenely, eyes closed, in a chair by the fireplace of a friend with whom he was staying for several days after our board meeting. Dr. V. was deep in meditation, his daily habit. A longtime disciple of the Indian sage Sri Aurobindo, Dr. V. begins his days at Aravind Hospital at 6:30 a.m. by going to a meditation room there for "a silent talk with God."

He asks to be a better tool for the divine force, to be able to overcome the afflictive emotions and instincts, like anger and greed, jealousy and egoism, which all too often can make the loftiest enterprises founder. And he asks to be able to find just the right way to show compassion to each of the patients he will see that day—to meet soul-to-soul.

For though it is an eye care hospital, under Dr. V.'s guidance the philosophy at Aravind is to care for the total person, to offer comfort and solace as well as excellent medical care. For example, patients' families are welcome to stay with them at the hospital, rather than having patients face their surgery isolated and alone. In that philosophy there is a lesson for medicine in the West, which seems to have seized on methods for assembly-line cost efficiency at the expense of humane care.

Those lessons will soon be shared. The Aravind Hospital is now starting an international institute for training in community ophthalmology, which will train teams from developing countries worldwide. People in public health and eye care will come to Madurai to learn the community eye-care techniques Dr. V. and his team have evolved—innovations such as mobile eye camps that bring sight-restoring surgery to the blind in even the remotest of villages. And beyond these innovations in technique, those who come to train at Dr. V.'s center will take home the philosophy of total care, from eye to soul.

Daniel Goleman

INTRODUCTION

*T*he theme of Harvard Divinity School's Wit Lectures, living a spiritual life in the contemporary age, reminds us of the inevitable tension that exists between spiritual values and our secular, contemporary culture. Harold M. Wit, Harvard College Class of 1949, was acutely aware of this tension when he established the lectureship with a generous gift in 1988. Its purpose, Mr. Wit wrote, would be "to bring to the Harvard community unusual individuals who radiate in their thought, word, and being those spiritual qualities and values that have been so inspiring and encouraging to me along my path. This in the hope that those listening to the lectures and being privileged to be in the good company of such persons might likewise be inspired and encouraged."

It was, indeed, a privilege to be in the good company of the Wit lecturer for 1991, Dr. Govindappa Venkataswamy. Dr. Venkataswamy is a doctor whose life and work are integrated with deeply held spiritual beliefs in a way that is nothing short of remarkable. Born in 1918, he is the founder and director of the Aravind Eye Hospital in Madurai, Tamil Nadu, deep in southern India. Although he began his career as an obstetrician, he had to change his medical specialty when severe arthritis badly crippled his hands. Despite this physical challenge, he found that he was capable of the delicate procedures required for eye surgery, and since he became an ophthalmologist, he has personally performed more than 100,000 successful eye operations.

Dr. Venkataswamy served as a doctor in the Indian Army. He spent many years at the Madurai Medical College, a government school, where he eventually became head of the department of ophthalmology. In the course of his work he made many important discoveries about the health of the eye, and pioneered national programs to eradicate the blindness that is so prevalent throughout India. One of his most notable innovations has been the establishment of mobile eye camps that travel to rural villages to examine villagers' eyes, to diagnose and treat their diseases, and in many cases to distribute corrective eyeglasses right on the spot. Those who need operations are transported free of charge to and from the Aravind Eye Hospital, established by Dr. Venkataswamy in 1976 after he retired from government service.

Over the years Aravind has grown to enjoy an international reputation for providing the best possible care efficiently and effectively, and for offering patients state of the art technology. Under Dr. Venkataswamy's direction, Aravind has become the largest and most productive eye-care institution in the world. It serves as an observation and training facility for medical residents and fellows from around the world, including the Massachusetts Eye and Ear Infirmary and the World Health Organization. In partnership with the Seva Foundation, a service organization based in California, Dr. Venkataswamy and Aravind are also establishing the Aravind Institute for Community Ophthalmology, which will provide training for eye-care workers from developing countries.

Aravind is notable for the compassionate spirituality that informs all it does. Its unique fee structure, for example, is arranged so that a third of its patients who can afford to pay for services subsidize the two-thirds who cannot. Patients, some of whom have never before been away from their villages, are housed with others from their own district so they do not feel isolated. Staff and visiting medical personnel are equipped, not only with exceptional surgical skills, but also with the value of selfless giving to others, a founding principle of the hospital. "Modern technology combined with spiritual consciousness is the need of the day," Dr. Venkataswamy has said, and many who visit

Aravind remark on the sanctity of its operating rooms.

Dr. Venkataswamy is a disciple of Sri Aurobindo (1872–1950), one of the twentieth century's most revered spiritual leaders, and someone who believed that an individual's spiritual evolution is linked to the rest of humankind, indeed, to the entire cosmos. Service to others is one of the pillars of this religious philosophy, and compassion is based on the spiritual realization, according to Dr. Venkataswamy, that "you are identified with whom or for whom you work. It is not out of sympathy that you want to help. The sufferer is part of you."

Dr. Venkataswamy's leadership and compassionate spirit have been recognized by a number of honors, among them the Padma Sri Award from the government of India, the Helen Keller International Award presented at the United Nations, and the Time-Life Service Award from the International Agency for the Prevention of Blindness.

What is the significance of spirituality for contemporary life? How are we to integrate our spiritual lives with our sense of vocation? I hope that in the life of this doctor, who is dedicated to village-level research into the causes and human costs of blindness in India and devoted to the eradication of curable blindness, and in the lectures on spirituality he delivered at Harvard Divinity School, you will begin to find the answers to these important questions.

Ronald F. Thiemann
Dean and John Lord O'Brian
    Professor of Divinity
Harvard Divinity School
Cambridge, Massachusetts

I

I am an eye doctor, a medical man trained in the rational and scientific way. There was no talk at all about spiritual consciousness in my medical training or practice. For the forty years that I have been in the medical profession, I have always talked to audiences about eye surgery and ophthalmology. So to be invited to a school of divinity to talk about spiritual life is very challenging, and I must thank Harold Wit for putting this task before me.

I was born to a farmer's family in a small village in south India, almost near the tip. The elders in the village told me that when my father was a baby a few months old, his parents and many of their neighbors died of cholera in one day. There was no school in my village. As small children we had to walk a mile and a half across a river to a village nearby. Every house had a buffalo, and the children had to take it out for grazing early in the morning. We came back home, had our gruel, and went to school. When we did get a school a few years later, we had no pencils or paper, not even a slate. We used to collect sand from the riverbed, spread it over smoothly, and write in it with our fingers. Later we were promoted to palm leaves, to write in script.

The school only went up to grade five, and most of the village children stopped their studies with that. Few dreamed of going on to higher studies. But my father was keen that I should continue, and he sent me to a nearby town where there was a high school. I was put up with a distant relative whose son was educated in the same school. But I fell ill constantly, and did not do well in the exams. The following year my maternal uncle, who worked as a clerk in a local office in the town, took me in, and I stayed with him and was educated for the next eight years. I finished school and did two years of college under his care. My uncles had been the first few from the villages to become educated and work in white-collar jobs.

My father also had the same sort of a schooling for two or three years. He was brought up in a deeply religious fashion, and used to have the Vaishnava caste mark put on his forehead every day. He would walk twenty-five miles each way to the temple of our family deity once in a month, carrying a pot of melted *ghee* [butter] on his head to offer to the Divine. It was a tradition in those families to have a teacher, a guru. The tradition was hereditary, so your son would become a disciple to your guru's son. My father's guru lived in the town near our family deity's place, and they had frequent contact. This sort of cultural background was strong in the history of our country. A guru, a kind of traditional school-of-divinity man, was there for every house; whether a king, a commoner, or a soldier, everybody had a guru to guide him in his earthly life, as well as life after death.

My father also spent his own time and money to plant hundreds of shade trees around pools and avenues in the village, and in the neighboring areas. He used to feed the poorer sections of our village with sumptuous meals. He built a hall with granite stone at a temple near our village. He built a modern house and was fond of using big granite boulders. He practiced good agriculture, and was far ahead of the people in the village. He was known for truthfulness and straightforwardness. People did not dare to tell him a lie. He aimed at perfection in all his works, and his children inherited this quality.

It was during the time that I was under the care of my uncle that Mahatma Gandhi was in the political forefront of the country, fighting for India's independence. His followers were everywhere, preaching and practicing his teachings. As small schoolboys we started spinning yarn with hand *charkas* or spindles. We shared the spindles to thread our yarns, and we boycotted foreign goods. There was picketing in front of indigenous liquor shops and shops selling foreign goods, and the police used to beat the demonstrators and put them in jail. My father started wearing *khadi*—homespun cloth—and I also started wearing it.

Gandhiji's ideas of celibacy, non-violence, truthfulness, and simple life appealed to a large number of people in the younger generation. There was a sense of communal harmony, and several national industries were started. His movement was not just political, and he was not just a political man. There was also an effort to revive the traditional *dharma* or culture of ancient India. The *Bhagavad Gita* became popular, and people started reading it to understand *karma yoga*. A lot of natives, who were only villagers, common people, were attracted by Gandhiji, not as a political leader, but as a sage and a saint. They revered him and almost worshipped him as a divine being. Plenty of them went to prison because Gandhi told them to go to prison. Millions courted imprisonment for the cause, and gave up all their earthly possessions to join him in his ashrams. Because of Gandhi, ordinary folk from villages were able to face and get rid of their fear of British colonial power, even though it meant imprisonment. Can you imagine people who had nothing to fall back on leaving their children and families, taking to the streets, and going to prison by the thousands? Institutions were started all over the country to spread Gandhi's message, and to educate children in his ideas and the basics of work-related education. Gandhi worked incessantly for the social and economic improvement of the down-trodden people in society, and all this had a great impact on our lives and thinking.

Gandhiji was not for renouncing the world to seek the Divine. Rather, he was for living and transforming life to reach the Divine. This notion shaped some of us, and we used to be called Gandhi-ites. Gandhiji talked constantly of "soul force," and he used it for all problems in the lives of individuals and institutions, and in politics. On several occasions he fasted for long periods—twenty-one days—to achieve communal harmony and self-purification, which he said would help to create harmony and better understanding.

His great strength was his capacity to love people. People who had views diametrically opposed to his went to him, and he gave them great respect, not as a diplomat, but as a loving soul. Though he fought against the British, he had several British disciples and good British friends. He had no hatred for British people, though he was against colonialism. You do not see this among political leaders today. Gandhi wanted no part of anything that was used to exploit others, whether it was mechanized industry or bureaucracy. He lived in this century, yet he practiced most of the teachings of Jesus Christ, especially loving your enemy, and he demonstrated that humanity can be lifted up to high levels of ethics and tolerance.

In 1942, when the "Quit India" movement began, I was in medical school. All of the students wanted to hoist the National Congress Party flag over our dormitories at that time, but the British were still ruling, and only the Union Jack was allowed to fly. So the British authorities told us to vacate the dormitories, and we all left to stay in private, rented places. All of this was done without any violence or hatred. It was wonderful to watch how millions of people had the courage and the tenacity to undergo all the suffering they endured, without ill will.

Everyone knows the bloodshed we experienced between Hindus and Muslims after India's partition. There are several episodes like that in human history. The human consciousness goes up, and people do heroic things. We witness wonderful creations in literature, art, music, and architecture, but then there is degeneration, and people seem to lose contact with the higher consciousness. This is the cyclical change in human history. But in our early days Gandhiji was all in all for us. He said one can make spiritual progress in this life, not by going to a monastery or an ashram, but by living the life of *Gita*, in politics, in business, in all facets of life.

I remember well reading the *Bhagavad Gita* in those days. I wrote to a friend of mine that I would like to practice yoga and be a yogi some day. But I didn't understand it then. At the same time Swami Vivekananda became very popular with us. His speeches were so powerful and inspiring they made me look forward to doing something challenging and great. My father had many of his books, and I began reading in them about traditional religious culture and philosophy. In my college days I started reading his *Raja Yoga*. His speeches and writings inspired millions of people in the world, especially in India, to realize the spiritual teachings of the Indian masters. He was a great force in the building of modern India. I also read the teachings of Sri Ramakrishna Paramahamsa, who had very little schooling, but who had known God in person. Occasionally I visited the Ramakrishna *Mutt* [ashram] in Madras to listen to the discussions, and for several years I used to practice *yogasanas* [bodily postures].

All these contacts influenced our thinking greatly in those days. We were not thinking of amassing money as our goal in life. We always aspired to some perfection in our lives, like the realization of God, or the reaching of higher levels of consciousness in yoga. But even though we had the deeply traditional culture of India, and the great spiritual influence of Mahatma Gandhi and Swami Vivekananda, materialism took over very powerfully, partly because religion went to extremes of oppression. In the name of religion there was much exploitation. In the name of religion many spiritual leaders were treated badly. The socially downtrodden were not allowed to walk in the streets of the city. They were not allowed to go into the temples. There were more decrees and dogmas, and some tried to exploit the name of religion to make money. All this provided a very good environment for secular materialism.

At about the same time the Russian Revolution declared that religion was just the opiate of the people. People took to this view very powerfully, and in my country the younger generation all became rationalists. They were able to take power from the Congress Party, which was Gandhi's party. Today, with modern satellite communications, I think people are becoming more and more rational and materialistic. If you go and ask young people at a university in India what their ambition is, they will say, "I would like to go to the Harvard Business School." They have not heard about Harvard Divinity School, which is much older. That seems to be the trend. In a country where millions of people courted imprisonment, and fought non-violently, the fate of India today is so much violence, so much corruption. People seem to have degenerated overnight. Whatever values we had just thirty or forty years ago seem to have disappeared entirely in the course of those years. What can we do? That is the challenging question raised by these lectures on living a spiritual life in the contemporary age, and I think it faces each of us in all parts of the world.

In 1944, after medical school, I joined the British army for a few years and served in several parts of India and in Malaysia. But in 1947 I developed severe arthritis, and I was discharged in 1948. I joined the maternity hospital in Madras for post-graduate training, because I had lost three cousins to a condition called eclampsia. All of them died in the last three months of their pregnancies. I was anxious to become an obstetrician, to do something to prevent other women from dying in the same way. But after a few months, because of the rheumatoid arthritis, nearly all my joints were severely swollen and painful. I was in a Madras hospital for over a year. I could not hold anything. I could not sit up. Severe pain has been my companion since then, and it has never left me. The arthritis crippled me badly, and for years I could not walk long distances, something I was accustomed to doing as a village boy. In the acute stage, for several months I could not stand up, and I was confined to bed.

I still remember the day I was able to stand on my feet. A relative had come to see me in the hospital ward, and I struggled hard to keep my feet on the ground and stand close to the bed without holding on. When I did, I felt as though I was on the top of the Himalayas. For several years I used to struggle to walk a few yards or squat down on the floor. Even now in villages we normally squat on the floor when we eat, and I find it difficult. I could not hold a pen with my fingers in the acute stage of arthritis. We normally eat our food with our fingers, and I found it difficult to take the food with my swollen fingers.

I drifted away from my interest in maternity, and I joined the eye hospital. I trained slowly to hold the knife and cut the eye for cataract operations. After some years I could stand for a whole day and do one hundred operations or more at a stretch. Eventually I learned to use the operating microscope and do good, high-quality cataract and other eye surgeries. On one side my father had taught me perfection. On the other side I was struggling hard with arthritis. My brain was always clear, but my hands were crippled, and it was not easy for me to walk even ten yards.

While all this was going on in Madras, a Gandhi-ite friend of mine said, "Let's go to the ashram in Pondicherry and have the *darshan* [sacred sight] of Sri Aurobindo." It was April, 1950. India had freedom, but Pondicherry did not, and we had to get passports to enter Pondicherry. It was my first *darshan* of the masters, and Sri Aurobindo passed away that year in December. People were able to see him once every three months, and there was usually a big crowd, about two thousand people. You marched in a line, you saw him for a second, and then you marched off. That day in April he did not make any sort of impact on me worth remembering, but some of the people who had come with me said they had seen the Divine. I could not understand what they meant at the time. I went back to Madras and started working in the eye hospital. I had some patients from Pondicherry ashram, and we became friends. I started visiting the ashram regularly for every *darshan*. People from the ashram used to come and stay with me, and gradually, over the years, I read Sri Aurobindo's books and became involved with his teachings.

Sri Aurobindo was born in Bengal in 1872. As a small boy he was sent to England with his brothers for schooling. He returned to India and served the state of Baroda from 1893 to 1906. In 1906, provoked by the partition of Bengal, he went to Calcutta, edited the periodical *Bande Matharam*, and became a leader of the Nationalist Party and the fight for freedom. It was at this time that he had his spiritual experiences. He could realize his spiritual self. He made spiritual progress very quickly, and began writing about his spiritual experiences. The British were afraid to have such a powerful writer opposing them. He advocated violence and trained people to fight the British. So a case was brought against him, and he was imprisoned in a solitary cell.

Once Sri Aurobindo gave a talk about his experience in jail at a place called Uttarpara. He said:

When I was arrested and hurried to the Lal Bazar Hajat, I was shaken in faith for a while, for I could not look into the heart of His intention. Therefore I faltered for a moment and cried out in my heart to Him: "What is this that has happened to me? I believed that I had a mission to work for the people of my country and until that work was done, I should have Thy protection. Why then am I here and on such a charge?" A day passed, and a second day and a third, when a voice came to me from within: "Wait and see." Then I grew calm and waited. I was taken from Lal Bazar to Alipore, and was placed for one month in a solitary cell apart from other men. I remembered then that a month or more before my arrest, a call had come to me to put aside all activity, to go into seclusion and to look into myself, so that I might enter into closer communication with Him. I was weak and could not accept the call. My work was dear to me and in the pride of my heart I thought that unless I was there, it would suffer or even fail and cease; therefore I would not leave it. It seemed to me that He spoke to me again and said, "The bonds you had not the strength to break, I have broken for you, because it is not my will that I have brought you here, to teach you what you could not learn for yourself, and to train you for my work. Then he placed the *Gita* in my hands. His strength entered into me, and I was able to do the *sadhana* [religious discipline] of the *Gita*. I was not only to understand intellectually but to realize what Sri Krishna demanded of Arjuna and what He demands of those who aspire to do His work, to be free from repulsion and desire, to do work for Him without demand for fruit, to renounce self-will and become a passive and faithful instrument in His hands, to have an equal heart for high and low, friend and opponent, success and failure, yet not to do his work negligently...it was while I was walking that his strength again entered into me. I looked at the jail that secluded me from men and it was no longer by its high walls that I was imprisoned; no, it was Vasudeva [Hindu lengendary king and Krishna's father] who surrounded me. I walked under the branches of the tree in front of my cell, but it was not the tree. I knew it was Vasudeva. It was Sri Krishna whom I saw standing there and holding over me his shade. I looked at the bars of my cell, the grating that did duty for a door, and again I saw Vasudeva. It was Narayana [a personification of solar and cosmic energy] who was guarding and standing sentry over me. Or I lay on coarse blankets that were given to me for a couch and felt the arms of Sri Krishna around me, the arms of my friend and lover. This was the first use of the deeper vision He gave me.

Sri Aurobindo egotistically thought he was to be the country's liberator, and he could not imagine what would happen to India and to politics without him. But when he asked the Divine, "Why have you thrown me in jail?" he realized it was divine power that had interned him, to teach him some of the spiritual values of life. In

23

a small cell Sri Aurobindo experienced what he calls the Divine Consciousness. In the gratings of a prison wall he saw the Krishna consciousness. In a tree in front of his cell he saw the arms of Krishna floating over him. The rough blankets were the hands of Krishna caressing him. In that miserable existence he had the Divine Consciousness, and that experience became very important for his later life.

Sri Aurobindo's companion in his work in Pondicherry was the Mother, who was born in Paris in 1878. Her parents belonged to a respectable family from Egypt. She had spiritual experiences at a young age, and then came to Pondicherry and met Sri Aurobindo in 1914. On the day of their first meeting, she wrote in her diary, "It matters not if there are hundreds of beings plunged in the densest ignorance. He whom we saw yesterday is on earth. His presence is enough to prove that a day will come when darkness shall be transformed into light, when Thy reign shall indeed be established upon earth." She joined Sri Aurobindo, accepted him as her guru, and followed his spiritual guidance. She left Pondicherry in 1915, returned in 1920, and remained physically present there until she left her body.

Like all seers and saints, Sri Aurobindo and the Mother taught that there is a divine part in man. Sri Aurobindo emphasized the future evolution of man, and said that the human mind is not the final step in that evolution. Evolution does not stop with man. We all accept that life began once, somewhere. Life entered inanimate matter, and progressed through various stages. There will be several more stages until what Sri Aurobindo called a new consciousness is reached. This supermind or supramental consciousness will transform the body, the mind, and the other life forces (what Sri Aurobindo called "the vital") of every human to a new type of being, entirely different from the present human being. For forty years it was Sri Aurobindo's task at Pondicherry to bring this supramental consciousness down to earth.

We all know that scientists have been able to discover electricity. Yet electricity was there all the time. We have been able to develop the technology to communicate from space down to the earth. We have been able to create atomic power. So also there is a Divine Consciousness that Sri Aurobindo was able to bring down to earth. Like electricity, like space technology, this Divine Consciousness is already permeating the world with its light and truth. The supramental being will have what we call Truth Consciousness, without groping in darkness, and will have the capacity to put knowledge to work in harmony with all around it. The human mind and body and life forces will all be changed. Life forces can be lower ones like selfishness, greed, jealousy, anger, or hatred. They can also be higher ones like love, compassion, and courage. But the whole being will have to change in order for man to become more perfect. Even the body has to be more perfect, so that an entirely new creature will result. The transformation will be like the difference between a man who lives in a cave, and modern man with all his scientific gadgets.

The goal of life, Sri Aurobindo also taught, is not to escape from the world to some higher heaven, but to transform life on earth into a divine life. This process is accomplished, not by the mind, but by surrendering the mind and the vital life forces to the Divine—allowing the divine force to work on the body, the mind, and the life forces, and to transform them. There are steps to the development of the mind, and Sri Aurobindo called the stages: the higher mind, the illumined mind, the intuitional mind, the overmind, and the supermind.

Every person has a psychic being or a spark of the Divine, but it is concealed by the ego's physical and mental consciousness. Evolution in nature is a slow process; it has taken millions of years for human beings to evolve. With yoga, this process can be hastened to occur within a lifetime, or a few lives. Sri Aurobindo said that rebirth after death is a natural process for the development of the psychic being. The purpose of rebirth is for the psychic being to evolve and experience different levels of consciousness until it becomes one with the Divine.

What I am really talking about is spiritualism. Spiritualism is a progressive awakening to the inner reality of our being, to a spirit, a self, a soul that is something other than our mind, body, and life. Spirit is an inner aspiration to know, to enter into contact and union with the greater reality beyond, a reality that also pervades the universe and dwells in us. As a result of that aspiration, contact, and union, there is a conversion, a turning, a birth into a new being.

Spiritualism is the antidote to our present crisis. The scientific pursuit, in its cold and even way, has made discoveries that have served a practical humanitarianism on one side, and on the other side has supplied monstrous weapons to egoism and mutual destruction. Science has made possible gigantic efficiencies of organization for the economic and social amelioration of the nations, but it has also turned that amelioration into a colossal battering ram of aggression, ruin, and slaughter. It has given rise on one hand to an altruistic humanitarianism, and on the other hand it has justified a godless egoism, a vulgar will to power and success. Science has drawn humanity together and given it new hope, but it has also crushed humanity with the burden of monstrous commercialism.

Sri Aurobindo said that the turmoil and disorder of the world needs to be replaced by a commitment to the power of a higher, truer consciousness. "One must…make a leap forward," he wrote. Yet despite the rich traditions of spiritual seers and people like Gandhi, there is much violence and crime in the name of religion in India. A narrow religious spirit often oppresses and impoverishes the joy and beauty of life. Religion, when it identifies itself only with a creed, a cult, a church, or a system of ceremonial forms, may well become a retarding force. In the name of religion women were treated badly. In the name of religion socially backward classes were deprived of basic rights. In my state of Tamil Nadu, a strong rational movement developed, and that movement is in political power even now. With our mass communications systems, a materialistic culture spread rapidly all over the world, and younger generations now think that material existence is the only reality.

Sri Aurobindo's essential method was to try to quiet and calm the mind. Then it could face both good and bad with equanimity. Every day I pray in the morning that I will not lose my temper. But then I go to the hospital, something happens, and anger seems to possess me. You know how anger can possess you; you cannot put anything else inside you when you are angry. There is no room for love or compassion. Sri Aurobindo said that unless you get rid of this anger, the higher forces cannot come to you.

I have constantly tried to experience the

peace and calmness that form the basis for *sadhana*. I experience it, but it is so transitory that I seem to lose it in no time. I remember when the Mother at Pondicherry gave a balcony *darshan* at six o'clock in the morning every day. When I went to Pondicherry, this early morning *darshan* was a must for me, even when I reached the ashram late in the night. It gave me the necessary energy and peace for the day. So I still visit the Aravind hospital meditation room every day, morning and evening, but my surrender is not complete enough to allow the Mother's force to stay and work in me. I live in my own superficial consciousness with its small attachments and prejudices. Even if another person has selfish motives, I must be able to place myself firmly in peace and *samata* [equanimity], and return love without expecting gratitude in return.

I want to radiate love and goodwill on all occasions, without giving any place in my consciousness to pride or prejudice. I want to love the patients and staff uniformly all the time. But I know that I create a sense of fear in my staff if they come late, or if they are not efficient in their work. This has become a strong habit with me, as I have been keen to maintain discipline in work. I should have tried love and kindness rather than instilling fear in them. I find that when people are not effective in maintaining discipline, morale declines, and the quality and quantity of work also decline rapidly. It would be ideal if discipline could be maintained with love and kindness. But when some people have complete freedom to act, they degenerate very quickly. They still need some amount of external force to maintain discipline. If people could grow into the higher consciousness and act from the higher level, they could influence others. Real discipline will come only when people are motivated by spiritual force.

I like to watch people and try to observe their consciousness. Similarly, I watch my own mental and emotional feelings and reactions. It is interesting to watch how alcohol or anger gets hold of people. Normally many of us are caught up in these lower "vibrations," or we live in our own small, narrow worlds. Only a very few of us become aware of higher levels of consciousness above the mental, the physical, the emotional. We cannot expect everyone to become spiritual, just as we cannot expect everyone to become a research scientist. We have to provide opportunities, facilities and help for people inclined to spiritual experience. That is what ashrams in India are supposed to do for spiritual seekers.

At Aravind we are deeply interested in getting people to pursue spiritual practices. The hospitals demonstrate that eyesight can be restored to all people irrespective of social or economic status, if we can combine modern technology and management with spiritual

practice. When we grow in spiritual consciousness, we identify ourselves with all that is in the
world, and there is no exploitation. It is ourselves we are helping; we do not act out of some
feeling of doing good to some poor, deprived
person. Human beings must change, and Sri
Aurobindo said that the Divine will bring about
the next step in the evolution human consciousness needs to undergo. What we need are "laboratories" where people interested in the progress
of spiritual consciousness will have opportunities to work. All over the world good scientists
work in laboratories seeking new discoveries in
the physical sciences. Similarly we need laboratories where people can pursue spiritual path-
ways. Throughout history, India has produced
spiritual people who, since the days of Buddha
or even earlier Vedic ages, have produced centers of spirituality to continue the tradition.
There are people genuinely interested in spiritual experience, and we must encourage them.

Normally, people think of spiritual or religious practice as a means to attain salvation or
heaven. They think that spirituality is for old
age, after you have had your share of life's plea-
sures by whatever means. But spiritual discipline and practice can enhance the capacity of
the body, mind, and heart, and make them better
tools. Some of the people who came under the
yogic influence of Sri Aurobindo and the Mother
of Pondicherry became poets and artists; others

were cured of illnesses. Others had spiritual experiences of a very high order, like reaching nirvana or experiencing the overmind. Spiritual life is not reserved for life after death only; its purpose is to make the present life rich in all aspects. The Mother of Pondicherry worked on the cells of the body to transform them. She and Sri Aurobindo guided people to advance in their spiritual consciousness and ascend to the level of the supermind. In the work at our own hospitals there is constant spiritual help and guidance at all levels. Our global effort to control blindness is the will of the Divine, and we pray to be made good instruments for that work. We want more people to join us in it, and to work for a life that is divine.

All of us must aspire, Sri Aurobindo said, for divine grace to work in us, for the opening of our consciousness to something higher. He advised us to reject all the qualities of the law of nature—lust or hatred or anger or ill will. It looks so silly, wanting love and good will for everybody. Instead we think, "That fellow cheated me yesterday; how am I going to feel love for him?" It is indeed a difficult task to practice love and good will in our daily lives. Yet it is especially important in our professional lives. Normally, said Sri Aurobindo, we react to things with our outer consciousness. We lose our tempers, for example. But if we step back a bit and watch with our inner being—all of us have an inner being—we will say, "Yes, I lost my head and talked very badly." If we try harder to get in contact with another person's inner being we will find near that inner being a soul—what Sri Aurobindo called the psychic being—in the heart's center.

Doctors have many patients to see. But do they really see the patient, or just the patient's wallet? Do they see whether the patient is a rich man who is going to pay them well, or do they see his soul and really become interested in his problems? Try to see a patient's inner being. It is a very, very interesting experiment. I used to see many rustic, unsophisticated, ordinary village men and women as patients. But when you contact their inner being, suddenly you seem to be one with them. They are not trying to determine your knowledge, or whether you are a qualified and capable doctor. What you see, rather, is a soul full of simple confidence: "Doctor, I accept whatever you say." There is an implicit faith in you, and you respond to it. You think, "Here is an old woman who has got so much faith in me I must do my best for her."

But how can I train myself to practice spiritual perfection? Once you separate your inner consciousness from your outer consciousness, you must try to realize your psychic being or soul, which can contact a deeper reality than your reason can. We have the opportunity to do this all the time, every minute, every second.

You can see from my arthritic hands that I had to learn how best to train my fingers to hold a surgical knife, when for years I couldn't even hold my pen. But I wanted to be the perfect surgeon. Sometimes I had to perform operations on hundreds of patients each day. How could I pray for the divine grace to do that and to get my physical body to help? What you need is the higher power to make your mind perceive truth. You want your life force to lose all hatred, jealousy and envy, and to look instead for courage and love. You want to surrender absolutely to the divine, to perfection, to whatever you may want to call it. You do not want anything egotistical within you. It is an experiment you are constantly conducting.

It has been my privilege to be in contact with several disciples at Sri Aurobindo's ashram and at other ashrams in India. I used to talk to them about hospital problems and family problems. Once I was upset about an incident, and I was angry and depressed for weeks. A disciple advised me to keep calm and not get perturbed over such incidents. He said that to remain quiet within, firm in the will to go through, refusing to be disturbed or discouraged by difficulties or fluctuations—that is one of the first things to be learned on the spiritual path. To do otherwise is to encourage the instability of the consciousness. Only if you keep quiet and calm can experience go on with some steadiness, though experience is never without periods of interruption and fluctuation. But these disturbances, if properly treated, can become periods of assimilation and the cessation of difficulty, rather than denials of *sadhana*.

Not to be disturbed, to remain quiet and confident, is the right attitude, but it is also necessary for me to receive the help of the Mother, and not stand back from her solicitude for any reason. One ought not to indulge ideas of incapacity or inability to respond, dwelling too much on defects and failures and allowing the mind to be in pain and shame on their account. In the end these ideas weaken you. If there are difficulties, stumblings, or failures, you have to look at them quietly, and in tranquility call persistently on divine help for their removal, not allowing yourself to become upset or pained or discouraged. Yoga is not an easy path, and a complete change of one's nature cannot be accomplished in a day.

The disciple from Sri Aurobindo's ashram who advised me about spiritual calm had more to say about yoga. He said that the whole meaning of the yogic consciousness is in its invisible force. Yoga does not bring merely a feeling of power without any result. It produces tangible inward and outward results. Who could be satisfied with such a meaningless hallucination and call it power? If we did not have thousands of experiences showing that the power within could alter the mind, develop the mind's powers and add new ones to it, influence human beings and things, control the conditions and functioning of the body, work as a concrete dynamic force on other forces, modify events, and so on, we would not speak of it as we do. Moreover, it is not only in its results but in its movements that yogic force is tangible and concrete. We can direct it, manipulate it, watch its movement, be conscious of its mass and intensity, in the same way we can be conscious of other perhaps opposing forces. All these things are possible and usual in the development of yoga.

Sri Aurobindo once wrote in a letter:

The yoga force is always tangible and concrete in the way I have described, and it has tangible results. But it is invisible—not like a blow given, or the rush of a motor car knocking somebody down, which the physical senses can perceive at once. How is the mere physical mind to know that it is there and working? By its results? But how can it know that the results were the results of yogic forces and not something else? It must be one of two things. Either it must allow the consciousness to go inside, to become aware of inner things, to believe in the experience of the invisible and supraphysical, and then by experience, by the opening of capacities, it must become conscious of these forces and see, follow, and use their workings, just as the scientist uses the unseen forces of nature. Or one must have faith and watch and open oneself, and then the mind will begin to see how things happen...In any field of work, certitude takes years of training and experience. To diagnose a disease with certainty takes time. But gradually you develop a sense of awareness about revelations, visions, and intuitive thoughts and ideas.

I was never an "idea" man. I always had to *do* something. In medicine we are practically involved in giving eyesight to someone, in relieving someone's pain. I completed my medical residency in a hospital in Madras, where the medical school, organized by the British, was over 170 years old. I stayed in Madras until 1956, when I was posted to the medical school in Madurai as head of the eye department.

Madurai is a town in southern India famous for the Meenakshi temple, the biggest temple in the world. It was built over the course of several centuries and can hold about a million people. The temple is in the center of town, and the streets are parallel to its walls. It is the center of the life of the people. Madurai has also been the center for Tamil language and culture since ancient days, and there have been three universities, one after another, since before the Christian era. Literature from the last ancient university remains, and you can still collect Roman and Greek pottery and coins, since there was also contact with them. It is said that the goddess Meenakshi, consort of Siva, was a queen and ruled the area. Lord Siva is said to have performed several miracles in Madurai. We have festivals in the city for nearly three hundred days of the year, and most of them remind us of the miracles Lord Siva performed.

The Madurai hospital was a district hospital, converted to a teaching hospital for the new medical school in 1954. I had the Madras model to copy, and an opportunity to build up the eye department and make it a center for training graduate students. I struggled hard with all my handicaps to strengthen this department. I was also exploring exactly how I could practice and perfect the spiritual methods of Sri Aurobindo in my own life and work—in eye surgery or diagnosis of eye disease—and in my way of dealing with patients.

After developing the eye department in Madras, in 1961 the state government gave us a mobile eye unit to organize eye camps and provide eye surgery for people who couldn't reach the hospital. The facilities we had at the hospital were meager, hardly fifteen or twenty beds, and we had thousands of patients to operate on. The government gave us a van, some staff people, and about fifty dollars for each cataract operation camp. I was lucky to have many of my Gandhian friends working in the government development department. We had nearly 200 patients to operate on at the very first camp, and we also had to feed them for a week before sending them home. Without asking, community leaders and volunteers came forward with enormous support, and fed the patients after the operations. It was a wonderful response, and the camps became very popular with the people.

In 1965 I was invited to the United States to learn about rehabilitation of the blind. We were going to begin a rehabilitation center for Madurai. It was an era of promoting rehabilitation of the handicapped. After World War II, there were many people who were handicapped, and modern methods were being developed to rehabilitate them. I didn't know anything about rehabilitating the blind, so I attended a conference in New York, where there is a world council for the welfare of the blind. There I saw how the blind were trained to move about with long canes. They learned to read braille and received vocational training. All this I had to learn.

In New York I also met Sir John Wilson, who founded the Royal Commonwealth Society for the Blind. He is blind himself, and I used to see him standing alone, waiting to have someone guide him to his room or to a bus. Most of the people at the conference were blind; I was one of the few sighted ones. So I used to offer my help to Sir John, and we came to know each other. I told him about our eye camps, and he suggested increasing their numbers with the help of the Royal Society. It was a very great gift for me, because my idea had always been to help my own village folk—honest, sincere people who for some reason had lost their sight but had no way of regaining it because the hospitals did not provide enough beds to take care of them.

We organized more and more camps, and once performed over 700 cataract operations in one day, a world record at the time. We gave patients free food and free spectacles. Sir John agreed to support additional eye camps if I could conduct them. Local industries and businesses gave us much support. In 1973 the government established the Chief Minister's Eye Camp Project, and we organized huge numbers of eye camps, restoring sight to thousands of people. All these projects brought great credit to the eye department at Madurai, and it became one of the top eye programs in the country. But it was not out of some sort of philanthropic feeling that I did something good for the people. It was more a feeling that they were one with me, part of me. I was not condescending to do something good for them, as though I were a superior being. Rather, I felt a part of me was suffering with them; I was suffering from what they were suffering.

A few years later Sir John and I went with another friend to see Indira Gandhi when she was the Prime Minister of India. Sir John talked to her about the problem of blindness, explaining that millions of people in India were blind, and we needed a national organization to control this blindness. She readily agreed, and gradually I was moving up from working in just a small hospital to overseeing a growing network of eye camps. As national consciousness about blindness grew, our own physical work increased.

More and more people joined us in our work, and the national consciousness kept widening to include many, many people. As Sri Aurobindo would explain it, spiritually you feel happy that you are no longer left inside your small, narrow ego and limited to concern only about your own life and your own family; you try to break that ego and widen your consciousness. You grow in spiritual consciousness.

Sri Aurobindo described the various levels of consciousness as a series of four ascending steps to the development of the mind. From the ordinary human mind you can move to a level he called the higher mind. Then you can advance to the illumined mind, then to the intuitive mind, and finally to the overmind. But the overmind is not wholly sufficient to transform our consciousness; the supermind alone is capable of achieving that. Let me try to describe each of these four steps.

Our first decisive step out of human intelligence and normal mentality is an ascent into a *higher mind*, a mind no longer marred by obscurity or half-light, a mind characterized by a large clarity of the spirit. There is a spontaneous, inherent knowledge in a higher mind. It is a mind of luminous thought, a mind of spirit-born knowledge. It is all-aware, and realizes its conceptions swiftly and effectively. That is the characteristic of this greater mind of knowledge, knowledge that is not acquired, but is a self-revelation of eternal wisdom.

This greater, more brilliant mind always works on the rest of the being, on the will, and on the heart and its feelings, on the life forces, and on the body itself through the power of thought or the force of ideas. Even in the body the idea works so that, for example, the potent thought and will of health replaces the body's faith in illness, its consent to illness. The idea of strength calls on the substance, power, motion, and vibration of strength; the idea generates the force and form proper to the idea, and imposes it on our substance. It charges the whole being with a new and superior consciousness, lays a foundation for` change, and prepares the whole being for a superior truth of existence.

The *illumined mind* is an even greater force. It is a mind no longer of just higher thought, but a mind of spiritual light. In the illumined mind the clarity of the spiritual intelligence subordinates itself to an intense luster, to a splendor and illumination of the spirit. The lightning and power of spiritual truth and power break from above into the consciousness and add to the wide enlightenment, the calm, and the vast peace that characterizes the larger spiritual principle. The illumined mind brings with it a fiery order of realization and a rapturous ecstasy of knowledge. A downpouring of inwardly visible light usually envelops it. The illumined mind does not work primarily by thought, but by vision. The consciousness of a seer is more powerful for knowledge than the consciousness of a thinker. The power of inner sight is greater and more direct than the power of mere thought.

The *intuitive mind* has four powers: a power of revelatory truth-seeing, a power of truth-hearing, a power of immediate truth-seizing, and a power of automatically perceiving the exact relation of truth to truth. Intuition can perform all the action of reason, including the function of logical intelligence, but it does so by its own superior process, and with steps that do not fail or falter.

The *overmind*, even when it is selective and not total, is still a power of cosmic consciousness. When the overmind descends, the predominance of the ego becomes entirely lost and finally abolished in a largeness of being. A wide cosmic perception and feeling of a boundless universal self replaces it. Our normal perception of things spiritual and things mundane is mental, but with the overmind there is a supreme and radical reversal of consciousness, and the standards and forms of ordinary mental cognition are no longer sufficient. Sri Aurobindo also called this mind a "mind of light," that is, a mind capable of living in truth and passing into the supermind, whose very essence is a consciousness and power of the infinite.

Now all of this is really like a medical description. We say we do an examination of a patient with the ordinary naked eye, and then we also do a microscopic examination, magnified a hundred times; we can see the tuberculus bacillus, or the leprobacillus. Then we move up to using an electron microscope, which magnifies 100,000 times. Using the microscopes is not unlike reaching your higher mind, moving beyond the ordinary mind which normally gropes in darkness and does not know the whole truth. But when you reach the higher mind you see nothing but truth, just like with a powerful microscope. That truth is still in the form of an idea. At the stage of the illumined mind it comes as a vision.

This is really not uncommon. Lots of us suddenly have an intuition. A scientist, a musician, an artist, a businessman—all of us are familiar with intuitions and inspiration. It is very difficult for us to explain where our intuitions come from, but one who has gone through this process realizes that they come from an illumined state of mind. People who work at developing their spiritual consciousness see higher and higher degrees of mind, thought, and ideas. Sri Aurobindo used to say that the poetry of

Milton came from this mental level. It is the equivalent of the appearance of an electron microscope. As you grow in the higher consciousness, not only is your knowledge greater, but you also reach a higher power and a higher bliss. All of us get ideas, but do they come from a higher mind, a higher region of consciousness, or from lower regions, from selfishness, greed, hate, and lust? Those lower ideas must be rejected.

All of us are familiar with the pressures of the body. Eating gives us happiness, and sleep gives us happiness. But as you grow in the higher consciousness, you are like a musician, a poet, or an artist enjoying something different from mere bodily pleasure. For some reason or other you experience an immense pleasure that is neither of the body nor of the mind. It seems to come from higher regions. I think all of us experience it sometimes. It is like seeing a building. If you built it, brick by brick, you have a more intimate knowledge of it, like the intimate knowledge a mother has of her child. The knowledge comes not from reason or the human mind, but from a different level of perception. And once you reach beyond these lower levels to the supermind, it is a divine region. All these things are there, but we are not aware of them. Only when we methodically grow in consciousness can we identify the various centers of consciousness.

One direction in which our consciousness must grow is an increasing hold—from within or from above—on the body and its powers, and its more conscious response to the higher parts of our being. As Sri Aurobindo wrote,

It is difficult to measure the degree to which the mind is able to extend its control or its use of the body's powers...and push back its human boundaries; it becomes impossible to fix any limits. Even, in certain realizations, an intervention by the will in the automatic working of the bodily organs seems to become possible...There are higher levels of the mind than any we now conceive, and to these we must one day reach, and rise beyond them to the heights of a greater, spiritual existence. As we rise we have to open to them our lower members, and fill these with those superior and supreme dynamisms of light and power; we have to make more and more of the body—even an entirely conscious frame and instrument, a conscious sign and seal of the power of the spirit.

Recently I asked some friends in the ashram about the graphic vision possible for the illumined mind, and they said it is just like a doctor who examines a patient and says, "This man looks beautiful, but unfortunately he has got diabetes," or "his lung is eaten by cancer." It does not look like that to an ordinary man. In the same way, people who have gone up the higher consciousness levels can use what they call spiritual mental force, just as a doctor uses the force of a laser. In the same way spiritual forces can be used to find out what cosmic forces are at work in the world.

There is a saint in the northern part of India. His name is Neem Karoli Baba. He was not educated in the conventional sense, but he is a real saint who has had many disciples in both the East and the West. One day he told an American doctor, Dr. Larry Brilliant, who had come as a disciple to his ashram, to join the United Nations medical forces and give small-pox vaccinations in the villages. Baba sent Dr. Brilliant to the World Health Organization (WHO) office in Dehli to work for the eradica-tion of smallpox, but at the time WHO had no job for him, and smallpox was not one of its pri-orities. Dr. Brilliant returned to the ashram, but Baba sent him back to WHO six times until he got the job and began working on smallpox. Dr. Brilliant had gone to Baba for spiritual knowl-edge and solace. He was surprised, to say the least, when his guru wanted him to join a pro-gram to eradicate smallpox. He had never even seen a case of smallpox, but his guru told him everything about the disease in great detail: where it was located in India, where the bad epi-demics were and in what seasons, what the transmission cycles were—everything about the epidemiology. The guru said, "this is the divine's gift for human labor, that smallpox

47

must be eradicated from the world." Once Dr. Brilliant was admitted to the WHO program, orders arrived from the WHO central office to tackle smallpox with a prevention program.

See how forces that are not normally visible to us are visible to people when they grow into higher consciousness, and see how universal forces work? They are able to guide us, and a disease like smallpox begins to be eradicated. At one level of consciousness, Dr. Brilliant's getting the job looks like a miracle to us. At another level it is something common, not a miracle. Once you assume a higher spiritual conscious-ness, what happens is a natural, common thing, whether it is a healing by Christ, or a healing by somebody else. It is not unlike seeing oil under the ground from a satellite. To me it might look like a miracle. But to a scientist, it is quite possi-ble to find gas or oil deep under the soil, or to forecast the weather. In the same way, when you grow into higher consciousness, you are able to see world forces very commonly, just as you in this audience see me. We may be unable to see the inner forces that are at work on the cosmic level, or even the individual level. But it is the common experience of people who reach that higher consciousness to discover a vision of truth, and they can see things very clearly. Sometimes it is not uncommon even for people like us to experience something very, very close to us, but we do not know where it comes from.

The more the mind becomes absolutely quiet, the more it sees the higher force.

I once asked a friend who had lived at the ashram in Pondicherry for fifty years to show me someone who was in contact with his soul all the time. I wanted to know how to recognize such a person. My friend took me to someone at another ashram nearby, and the minute I sat in the place where he was meditating, I saw something like a solid piece of matter enter me. I was a little bit afraid of it. But I felt nothing, so how could it be? Even a scientist knows you can not concentrate so much on one thing, whatever you do, that you can keep everything else in you quiet. But if you can keep the mind absolutely still, it is a very, very peculiar experience. You will find that it *is* possible for higher forces to come into contact with such a mind. Spiritualists are accustomed to using yogic force for many things, including curing illnesses and social problems. You cannot see electromagnetic forces, but you can see a scientist manipulating gadgets and putting instruments to use. It is the same with people who have the higher spiritual consciousness. They can even know when someone else is ill. Once my brother-in-law suddenly suffered acute jaundice and fever, and an old man, in the ashram a hundred miles away, spoke of it. He was able to recognize it through the force of the higher consciousness.

How can we recognize and interpret the

divine guidance that can come to us through circumstances, experience, and relations with others? If you want to follow a discipline of yoga, before you do anything you must try to discern if the inspiration received is real, if it comes from the Divine, or if it is simply a reaction to outer consciousness, a mere mental or emotional impulse. It is very important to try to discern and then act in full knowledge of the cause. But there are very many things we do that we are not in the habit of thinking about beforehand. The only thing that matters is the attitude with which they are done. Getting married, going to live in one place or another—these things are generally considered to have far-reaching consequences and to be important, and they are, to a certain extent. But from the point of view of yoga, everything depends much more on the attitude one takes than on the outer action itself. And so the importance of all the very small acts of daily life is reduced to a minimum.

When we are very attentive and very sincere, we can have an inner yet perceptible indication of the value of what we undertake, the value of the action we are doing. For someone whose goodwill is entire, who is sincere with the whole conscious part of his being, who wants to do the right thing in the right way, there is always an indication. If for some reason or other, one launches upon a more or less fatal action, one always feels uneasiness in the region of the solar plexus. The unease is not violent, and it does not compel dramatic recognition. But it is very perceptible to someone who is attentive. It is something like regret, or lack of assent. It may go as far as a kind of refusal to collaborate. It makes no noise, it does not hurt. It is at the most a slight uneasiness. If you disregard it, if you pay no attention, if you attach no importance to it, after a little while it completely disappears.

Almost every day of my life I saw a child who had gone blind due to malnutrition. When children born normally are deprived of food and protein and vitamin A, overnight their eyes seem to melt, and they become blind. When Sir John Wilson and I went to see Indira Gandhi, we told her that almost a hundred thousand children were going blind in her country. Now nearly a quarter of a million children all over the world are going blind due to vitamin A deficiency. From the earliest days of my career as an eye doctor, I have been deeply distressed to see young children going blind due to vitamin deficiency. When I began my career at the government hospital in Madurai in 1956, I also began research in vitamin A. In 1971, with the help and support of the Royal Commonwealth Society for the Blind, I established a nutrition rehabilitation center in the hospital. I wanted to continue this work to prevent nutritional blindness in children when I retired. Since there was a threat that the center would be closed, in 1984 I began the Aravind Children's Hospital.

This hospital has not established itself as a pioneer institution, nor earned a reputation for quality service like the Aravind Eye Hospital. In spite of all my efforts, I have not succeeded in the building of the hospital or the field work. But it is a good lesson for me to see how our efforts alone cannot succeed without Divine Grace. I have tried to motivate the staff to show compassion and kindness to the patients, but somehow we still have not succeeded. It is a constant reminder to me that however good I may be in one area, I can simply be a failure in another. There is always a greater need to surrender to Divine Grace.

I recall my trips to Jerusalem and Geneva for international meetings. Progress was slow and gradual. We were trying to grow from our narrow, limited selfish consciousness to a global consciousness, to attain a greater perfection in our work, but it happens slowly. Why am I telling you this? Because in spite of all the changes in our rational, material lives, there are concrete forces at work, forces we can see, like forces for world peace. In spite of many wars, people still talk about world peace and crave it. People still think about world pollution. Even schoolchildren talk about it.

With the descent to earth of the supramental force Sri Aurobindo spoke of, our own evolution will be more rapid. But in spite of all modern scientific devices and technologies, the core of the human mind, the inner consciousness, has not developed to meet everything that challenges us. Some say that there is going to be a collective change of conscience. Rapid progress has been made due to the conscious effort and mental powers of human beings.

Now a similar rapid progress has to occur in the inner consciousness also. Sri Aurobindo said that nature is going to lead us to a divine life. In the divine life there will be a divine body. The mind will not grope in darkness but it will be capable of seeing the truth, of being conscious of it. Just as we have electricity, computer technology, and hundreds of other things, so there will also be these things.

How can a school of divinity work to bring this about? Whether a man is poor or rich, black or white, whether he lives on this street or another street in the small village called Earth, these are our challenges. Sri Aurobindo mentioned how he used spiritual force in thousands of ways to cure illness, and to fight in World War II. Gandhi always talked about "soul force" in his struggle for freedom. He had a very powerful disciple, a very advanced spiritual man named Vinoba Bhave. Gandhi told the British government, "I am going to ask Vinoba Bhave to court imprisonment, as a demonstration against the ruling of a country like India by Britishers."

This is what they call in Hindu *satyagraha*, a single man fighting against a huge colonial empire by love, by spiritual force.

Vinoba was a unique man. After Gandhi died, he toured all of India on foot. He saw in one place that the communists had captured a place where landowners held all the property and thousands were landless. There was violent class struggle. Vinoba said, "No, this is the land of Gandhiji. No violence. Instead, non-violence and love." He persuaded the people who had land. He talked to them as human beings, as souls that had divinity in them, and said, "These are your brothers and sisters. Share your land." That began a very big experiment called the Bhoodan or Land Gift Movement. Vinoba was able to take millions of acres of land from people and distribute it to the powerless in India. So these are two examples: Gandhi, who used his soul force to fight the British Empire without violence, without hatred or ill will, making people resist simply by their moral courage and soul force, and Vinoba Bhave, who launched a large movement.

I will conclude with one final example of how Sri Aurobindo used a higher spiritual force to do battle. He described his experience during World War II: when it appeared that Hitler would crush all the forces opposed to him, and Nazism would dominate the world, Sri Aurobindo began to intervene. He declared himself publicly on the side of the Allies, made some financial contributions in response to appeals for funds, and encouraged those who sought his advice to enter the army or share in the war effort. Inwardly, he put his spiritual force behind the Allies from the moment of Dunkirk, when everyone was expecting the immediate fall of England and the definite triumph of Hitler. Sri Aurobindo had the satisfaction of seeing the rush of the German retreat; their military victory was almost immediately arrested, and the tide of the war began to turn. He did this because he saw that behind Hitler and Nazism were dark, satanic forces. Their success would mean enslavement to the tyranny of evil, and a setback to the spiritual evolution of mankind. It would also lead to the enslavement not only of Europe, but of Asia, an enslavement far more terrible than any India had ever endured and the undoing of all the work that had been done for her liberation.

That is how spiritual force works.

II

Spiritual growth is evolutionary. Our minds and mental consciousness are not the culmination of that evolution, however. There is another stage, the stage of the supramental consciousness, that Sri Aurobindo worked to bring down to earth.

It is said that there have been hundreds and thousands of spiritual giants on earth, but that it was never the opportune time for this new force to come to earth. Once the supramental force does come down to the earth, there is going to be an accelerated evolution of all things, whether in the physical sciences or in spiritual matters. At that next stage of development, our whole mental being will have to change. There will be a new body and a new mind. We will know light and truth and new life. This will be more than a divided consciousness. It will be more than the mere suppression of greed or lust or selfishness. There will be a complete transformation.

There was a time when people rode in coaches. When we shifted from coaches to automobiles, things changed completely. We could now travel at a hundred miles an hour. When the higher consciousness comes, we will need to change and perfect both the body and the spirit. When you are traveling in the air at 400 miles an hour, you need a different vehicle, a different "body," different gadgets, different tools of communication to control that body. So, when our consciousness levels improve, at each stage of improvement there is an improvement in the body. In the higher mind levels, the mind has to try to refine your emotions. It must try to get rid of your lower nature and perfect your body, just as athletes perfect their bodies in the Olympics. The higher mind has its own impact. It makes the body more perfect. It makes the mind more truthful. When you reach some higher, more illumined mind, changes occur. Just as with each new discovery on the earth—space communication, for example—the whole gamut of life changes. Everything becomes computerized. So, whenever a higher consciousness arrives, there is change. The changes may not come consciously. We may not consciously set out to computerize every machine, or to bring the illumined mind to our level. But we may try to do more perfect surgery, or to reorganize society, or to deal with current political conflicts. New forces are coming now. The old mind can suppress and hold down inferior mental concepts; only the new mind, the supramental one, can transform.

I have already spoken about all Gandhi did to lift the whole nation of India from violence to non-violence and love. But all of that is gone now. It was not permanent. Now in India we do not have the stability of that consciousness, and instead rationalism and materialism prevail. Yet it is possible to say that the whole material aspect of our being can be changed completely, and it is that process we must deal with now.

In 1976, I retired at age 58 from government service and my professorship at the medical school in Madurai. I had my pension, and I did not need more money, but I wanted to continue my serious work. I was already involved in the national program for the control of blindness. I began getting very involved in World Health Organization (WHO) programs as well, so one's consciousness does get wider and wider.

I also began a non-profit public charities trust, and under that trust I founded the Aravind Eye Hospital at Madurai in the name of Sri Aurobindo. I worked with my sister and her husband, who are also ophthalmologists.We began with ten beds, and gradually were able to expand to forty beds and build a low-cost/free hospital. I had little money at the time, and it was all somewhat improvised, but in a country where poverty is the main impediment, we had to improvise because we could not get any help from the government or from missions. Now Aravind has grown to become the biggest eye hospital in the world. Over 50,000 major eye operations are performed annually, and over two-thirds of them are done free for the poor. Poor villagers are screened in rural areas by hospital doctors and technicians, and people in need of surgery are transported free of charge to the hospital, given free food, free operations, free eyeglasses, and then taken back to their homes. All of this is financed with the revenues from paying patients, with no support from the state, though partial support for the free operations comes from international non-governmental agencies. We also offer specialty eye clinics which provide high-quality care. There are two branches of the Madurai hospital, one in Tirunelveli, one hundred miles to the south, and another at Theni, forty miles to the west. In these hospitals more than sixty percent of the work is done for free.

Today the Madurai hospital is also recognized for its residency training, and we train most of the staff we need. Residents from Chicago, Boston, New York and elsewhere also come to work and learn there. WHO sends eye doctors and ophthalmic technicians from neighboring countries for training in community ophthalmology. More than a dozen fellows are trained each year in a number of sub-specialities, and we help neighboring countries—Sri Lanka, Nepal, Maldives, Burma, Indonesia—by sending our senior staff there and by bringing their eye specialists to Aravind for training. We also train Tibetans from refugee camps as ophthalmic assistants, and they go back to work in their communities.

The effort to control needless blindness has become increasingly global in recent years. Some of the same workers from the world smallpox campaign embarked on a project in Nepal, hoping to eliminate blindness there in five years. The International Lions Foundation has initiated a "Sight First" campaign, and the American Academy of Ophthalmology started a program to support that global work. For developing countries, the Aravind model of providing free eye operations without state support seems an ideal example, and there is an effort to replicate the model in many parts of the world.

I have mentioned that I work with other members of my family. They have been a great support, and we are indeed something of a family operation. In India, we still have what I would call the joint family system, though it is gradually disappearing. I am the eldest in my family. My father died in 1950 when I returned home from the army. I was still suffering from acute arthritis. My two younger brothers and one younger sister were all studying; one sister who had finished school stayed at home to help my mother. It became my responsibility to support their educations, to arrange their marriages, and to help them settle in life. My mother was able to look after our farm with the help of my youngest brother; my father had groomed him for farm work even when he was very young. He used to buy the bullocks, sell the produce, and purchase whatever the farm needed. My other brother was in engineering school; he found a job in Madras when he was finished, and I became an assistant eye surgeon in the Madras hospital, so we lived together. By 1954 I had gotten one brother and one sister married. Eventually both brothers went to the United States for engineering studies and returned to India in 1964 to start a construction company. The company has built all the Aravind hospitals at cost, and my younger brother looks after the finances and gives most of his time to hospital management. Besides one sister and brother-in-law I already mentioned who are ophthalmic surgeons, my brother-in-law's sister and her husband are also ophthalmologists and work with us as specialists in pediatric and cornea ophthalmology. There are two more eye surgeons from the family at the hospital, and four more young doctors in training who are part of the family.

Some of the family members are also devoted to the Sri Aurobindo ashram, and this is a great support for the growth of the hospital. Many of them have visited other famous international eye institutes in Boston, Baltimore, Chicago, and Bethesda, Maryland, so that they can develop a vision for our own Aravind hospitals. Finally, one sister looks after our guest house, where we accommodate residents coming from the United States and other countries. All of this is a great asset for the future growth and maintenance of the hospitals.

In 1980 my friend, Dr. Charles Schepens, came from Boston and laid the foundation for a main building. I still did not have the money; the bank said that I was not credit worthy. So I had to mortgage my house and borrow 500,000 rupees to begin construction. The family construction company built the ground floor. One-third of the admissions were paying patients. With the revenues from the paying patients we could finish building the place, buy the equipment, and take care of the other two-thirds of the patients for free.

In addition to the high quality of treatment we offer, we are also trying to bring spiritual practice into our work. When the hospital building was opened in Madurai, we were able to obtain relics of Sri Aurobindo, who passed away in 1950. We have a meditation room, and though no one is compelled to go there, the room is visited by staff members and patients alike. The meditation room, and the desire of Aravind's senior staff members for divine guidance, have created an atmosphere of spiritual influence in the hospital. The senior nursing staff appreciates the atmosphere of serenity and quiet efficiency, and sets an example for the junior staff. Though Aravind eye hospitals do the largest volume of eye operations in the world, we seldom talk about it. We do not publicize the excellent work that goes on in the special clinic's retina vitreous unit, the IOL unit, and the cornea unit. It may take longer for people to know about us, but it is better to be slow and steady, and to aspire for perfection in our work. Sri Aurobindo promised that his consciousness would stay on the earth until the purpose for which he had come to the earth—the supramental evolution and firm establishment of supramental consciousness—was achieved. So there is a new power on the earth not contained in any ideology, and one we can communicate with just as we communicate with satellites. Some of us at the hospital go to the meditation room in the morning and evening. There is a force presiding there which seems to help us.

How exactly do you practice spirituality? When we started this hospital we were helped by the Seva Foundation. I have told you the story of Neem Karoli Baba and how he was able to see the divine will to eradicate smallpox. Some of those people who worked in the WHO smallpox program, left WHO once they eradicated the disease and went to aid the people at Aravind. Some of them work at the Centers for Disease Control. Some came to the Seva Foundation and said, "What can we do next?" They had done a mighty thing to eradicate smallpox. An idea came to them then to eradicate needless blindness from the world. I was happy to join, and we said, "Let us begin in Nepal and eradicate blindness in five years time."

The bulk of the people we treat are poor people, millions of them. They have nothing to fall back on except the support that their children can give them. They usually subsist on one meal a day, or sometimes nothing at all. A few years back we had a visit from a famous British health economist who had come to study us. We went every day and met some of the people who had been blinded by cataracts, and the economist asked them, "How are you?" They would reply, "I am fine." "When did you last eat?" he would ask. "Yesterday at noontime I ate," was the usual answer. "What about in the evening?" he persisted. "I can manage. I can eat again tomorrow," they would say. That meant they had nothing to eat. He asked them, "Well, how do you eat now?" "I washed my stomach today," they would say. He could not understand what they meant. I explained that they mixed what food they had with a lot of water so it filled their stomachs. That is what they called washing the stomach.

Now these people had worked all their lives, for fifty years or more. They had brought up and supported their families, and when they were afflicted with cataracts, life became really hard for them. Often the people we treat do not even have a mat on which to sleep. It is such a simple condition to change. Once you operate on the cataracts, people can see very well and do their jobs. Seva Foundation helps support the expense of transporting, feeding, and treating patients. Sometimes people come from hundreds of miles away. The cost of feeding a patient for six or seven days is only a dollar and a half. They do not eat more than that, and that is all they can afford.

Some of my friends have asked me how we have trained our staff people in "the Aravind culture." An industrialist from Delhi once came and said, "I need to build a hospital, and I am very much impressed with your hospital. Could you come and start a hospital in Delhi for me?" I asked, "What is it you want? You have all the money you need. It is not difficult for you to put up a hospital in Delhi. Why don't you do it?" He said, "No, I want a hospital with the Aravind culture. People are cordial here. They seem to respect people more than money. There is a certain amount of inner communion or compassion that seems to flow from them. How do you do it?"

We do not know how we do it, but it has been done. When we need technical assistants, we select girls from the villages—simple, honest people brought up in the traditional culture, which includes consideration for family and the community. Their families have provided a certain discipline, love and care in their daily lives.

They have not been urbanized. They are not interested in drugs and irresponsible sex. They can be easily trained to care for somebody else. Twice a year we find them and train them intensively. Whenever there is an opportunity, we take some of them to Sri Aurobindo's ashram at Pondicherry. The janitors are usually addicted to alcohol, and often they starve. The hospital provides a free midday meal for all of them, as well as clothing. But we have made the best use of the people who have come, and we built teams.

It has been a more difficult job to find the right doctors and medical professionals to join us. We have had problems with doctors who became drug addicts, and we sent them away. Some doctors join us from their residencies. We try to condition them gradually for longer hours of concentrated work. In some medical schools the training is poor, and the students are not accustomed to working for more than a few hours a day. At most hospitals the staff members work for a few hours and go home in the afternoon. When doctors are posted to primary health centers, they go to work only in the mornings, and only three or four days a week. Government office workers work only from 10:00 a.m. or later until 5:00 p.m., five days a week. Many government servants work only thirty hours a week. We normally work for eight to ten hours a day and six days a week. We want doctors to develop a helpful and kind attitude toward patients, especially poor villagers. The bureaucracy of government institutions intimidates people; that is a remnant of colonial rule. We regularly send our staff to village eye camps, where there is no fear or intimidation, and try to develop in them love and affection for the people. We create an opportunity for comradeship between the hospital staff and the villagers, and the staff can also observe the villagers' living conditions and aspire to improve them.

It does help that many of our doctors, nurses, and field organizers come from villages themselves. Rural people are well-informed about the urban community because of television. We insist on high quality care in diagnosis, surgery and all treatment, whether the patient is from a rural or an urban area. Some doctors are open to spiritual influence and appreciate the opportunity to work in Aravind eye hospitals. Others look only for financial or other benefits from the hospital. It is very difficult to get people really interested in the spiritual aspect of life. We do try to motivate our staff to achieve excellence in their surgery and publications, and some of them are internationally known for the quality of their work. Every opportunity to work—in Nepal, Maldives, or in Ganeshpuri—helps us to enlarge our vision and dedication. Our doctors are in demand for scientific paper presentations in other states of India; every opportunity to work and to keep this high quality in our work is my spiritual aspiration.

We also have tried to achieve the efficiency of a factory assembly line at Aravind. Four of our doctors assisted by twelve nurses could do about one hundred cataract operations in one day. This is something new to the ophthalmic world. How on earth do you set up to do a hundred operations? When visitors came and saw it, they were very happy. Although we are doing a large volume of operations, the quality doesn't suffer. We have a system and we can control its efficiency. This also helps to bring the cost down.

Because we had to go and bring patients to us, we had to organize about ten or fifteen mobile eye camps. In 1990 we were able to perform 50,000 major operations, and the hospital that began with twenty beds now has 1,500 beds. We receive no money from government agencies or programs, and we do feel that the higher consciousness is trying gradually to give us a system.

We are all aware of the parts of the human body as they work. We take in food, we eat, we like the taste of it. But after that, we wonder what goes on inside the body. Part of it is absorbed here, part of it is absorbed there. But we are not aware of it. The natural system of the body works, and it works wonderfully. The higher consciousness works in the same way; slowly, your system is built around it. It works itself out, but not according to human nature. Slowly, at the hospital we are building an organization which seems to be linked with the higher consciousness.

WHO has been monitoring us to see if the Aravind model can work in other developing countries. They have sent doctors from Indonesia, Sri Lanka, Burma, Vietnam and other neighboring countries. I remember especially one wonderful, talented young man who came from Sri Lanka. He was a very good surgeon, and at Aravind he realized that he could go back to his country and establish the same kind of organization. He went home, and in a month's time he secured enough voluntary support to do 500 operations in a week—something which just shook up the country. He asked that some nurses be trained at Aravind in order to form surgical teams. The same thing is happening in other countries. I do believe that, as an organization is gradually being built, you can try to open your consciousness to grow slowly and steadily to a higher consciousness, and to build from there.

Most of us have been taught about religion for the life after death—that we will go to heaven if we do certain things. Religion has often been about asceticism and mortification, about denying life here and now. But I say, lead a simple life. Don't regard the body as an obstacle. Instead, make it a better instrument. The most important thing about the supermind, the purpose of all the effort of supramental power, is to transform the existing human being, the body, mind, and life forces. This is a revolution that the earth needs badly. People who do not succumb to rationalism and materialism can perceive the possibility of a higher nature, a higher consciousness coming down to them. They will develop a better body and a better intellect.

We are all groping to find what can make the intellect sharper, to discover the truth clearly. Is it possible? Is it possible to find that power so that we can be transformed? Perhaps it is possible to work on this at a school of divinity. There, people are concerned with the lives of people. A business school gives the point of view of management and money. But we want to change the *core* of a human being, and we need organizations to help bring about the transformation. I think you constantly have to aspire to it. When I come to the United States, I tell my friends that this country has a wonderful capacity for organization, whether it is providing the basic needs of people, like food, shelter, transportation, and communication, or organizing various product industries and houses of business and commerce. You are able to deliver to the ordinary man his basic needs at a cost he can afford to pay. Now that is a wonderful system. Most communist countries did not succeed at it. Even though there is a profit motive, your system of organization has been powerful. I say that anybody can learn how to do it, and that the problem of blindness can be solved.

Is it possible to have a health delivery system? Everybody in America talks about the health care system. One side says it is costing the nation's economy too much money. Another side says there are many people who are unable to get care. I think the basic thing that we are all trying to do is organize. In America there are very powerful marketing devices to sell products like Coca-Cola or hamburgers. All I want to sell, to market, if you will, is good eyesight, and there are millions of people who need it badly. Nothing more basic is needed than good eyesight. A man who loses it loses fifty or sixty years of life. If that man can afford to pay me for it, certainly he should pay. If the man cannot afford to pay, still he needs eyesight. So how exactly should the market work?

At the same time I am also interested to see how people can grow in the higher consciousness so they will be happy. It looks like people with money are more unhappy than people who are faced with miserable conditions like starvation. In India I have seen people starving, or eating just one meal a day, and their only ambition is not to let this happen to their children. They just want to hold on to money so they can give it to their children. But in Western culture, where you are assured of your food, there are many people who are willing to challenge that. They are motivated by more than just holding on to money, and they will work, for example, in scientific laboratories, searching for truth in whatever their field. Who are the saints today? Perhaps they are the people working in laboratories in search of truth. Someone else may use them and their research, and may make money from it, but the real scientist is looking for truth. The search is so intense that perhaps he is willing to do it for little pay. The greatest satisfaction always comes from the truth.

There have been some attempts to replicate Aravind. The Royal Commonwealth Society of the Blind in England has a center to train leaders. There is also one in Baltimore, and many people come to them from developing countries. But then they find that the conditions prevailing here, and the sophisticated equipment, and the organizational methods, cannot be translated into reality in their own environments. A man coming from Africa, for example, finds it very difficult when an ordinary cataract operation in this country costs $3000. At home he has difficulty earning three dollars. Although the training in the West is highly sophisticated, it is not applicable to the developing countries. Instead, some countries send people to train with us in Madurai, to see the situation in another developing country.

A few years ago, Sight Savers planned to start an institute for community ophthalmology at Aravind, and recently the idea has been renewed. Ideas come from higher forces, constantly, to all of us. They also can come from our basic instincts and our lower natures. We must be careful to discern which ideas come from higher sources, and which do not. As we progress in opening up our consciousness to higher levels, we find that more ideas come to us. The idea for the institute was that it would be an opportunity for us to bring about the happy marriage between spiritual consciousness and modern technology—that is the challenge we face today. Aravind is a model for large-volume, self-supporting cataract surgery, appropriate for developing countries. They need well-trained leaders to plan blindness control programs suitable to different areas. They need training in epidemiology, biostatistics, health planning, operations research, health education, and social marketing. They also need to have an interest in spiritual practice.

We have wonderful modern technology. It allows us to see more than one thing at a time, to surpass the mind, which can always see only parts of things, never the totality. But the higher consciousness can always see the whole. Modern technology combined with spiritual consciousness is the need of the day. A supreme and total perfection is possible only by a transformation of our lower human nature, a transformation of the mind into a thing of light, and a transformation of life into a thing of power, an instrument of right action. Perfection is possible only by a happy elevation of our nature beyond its present comparatively narrow potential, becoming a self-fulfilling force of action and joy. There must be an equally transforming change of the body—a conversion of its actions, its functioning, its capacities as an instrument—moving it beyond the limitations which clog and hamper it, even its great present human attainments.

Sri Aurobindo wrote:

If the emergence and growth of consciousness is the central motive of the evolution, and the key to its secret purpose, then by the very nature of that evolution, this growth must involve not only a wider and wider extent of its capacities, but also an ascent to a higher and higher level, until it reaches the highest level possible. This would mean an entry or approach into what might be called a self-existent truth-consciousness in which the being would be aware of its own realities, and would have inherent power to manifest them in Time. All would be Truth, following out of its own unerring steps and combining its own harmonies. Every thought and will and feeling and act would be spontaneously right, inspired or intuitive, moving by the light of Truth and therefore perfect. All would express inherent realities of the spirit, some fullness of the power of spirit would be there. One would have surpassed the present limitations of mind. The mind would become a seeing of the light of Truth. The will would become a force and power of truth. Life would become a progressive fulfillment of the Truth. The body itself would become a conscious vessel of the Truth, part of the means of its self-realization, and a form of its self-aware existence.

Matter, after taking into itself and manifesting the power of life and the light of the mind, would draw down into itself the superior or supreme power and light of the spirit. In an earthly body it would shed its non-conscience and become a perfectly conscious frame for the spirit. A secure completeness and stability of the health and strength of its physical tenement could be maintained by the will and force of this inhabitant; all the natural capacities of the physical frame, all the powers of the physical consciousness, would reach their utmost extension and be there at command, sure of their flawless action. As an instrument, the body would acquire a fullness of capacity, a totality of fitness for all uses, which the inhabitant would demand of it far beyond anything now possible. These consequences of the truth consciousness descending and laying its hold upon matter would be a sufficient justification of evolutionary labor.

Light and bliss, beauty and a perfection of the spontaneous right action of the whole being are there as native powers of the supramental truth consciousness, and these will in their very nature transform mind and life and body even here upon earth, into a manifestation of the truth-conscious spirit.

The Mother of Pondicherry talked about a body totally different from the present one. Of Sri Aurobindo, whose entire body was, at the

76

end, suffused with a golden crimson hue, so fresh, so magnificent, she said, pointing to the light, "If this supramental light remains, we shall keep the body in a glass case." In our transformed bodies, procreation and digestion will take place without the present organs. If we can get people genuinely interested in growing in spiritual consciousness to come and work at the community institute, it would be wonderful, for Sri Aurobindo and the Mother have brought the supermind down to earth, and aspirants have to work for it. Our main work in the eye hospital is to repair parts of the body that are diseased, but gradually we have to open ourselves to the possibilities of new developments in the spiritual consciousness.

The Mother of Pondicherry also wrote of the supramental force in Sri Aurobindo:

He had gathered in his body a great amount of supramental force, and as soon as he left...you see, he was lying on his bed. I stood by his side, and in a way altogether concrete—with such a strong sensation as to make one think that it could be seen—all this supramental force which was in him passed from his body into mine. And I felt the friction of the passage. It was extraordinary, extraordinary. It was an extraordinary experience. For a long time, a long time like that. I was standing beside his bed, and that [the passing of the force into her body] continued. Almost a sensation—it was a material sensation. For a long time. That is all I know.

According to the Mother, there are two ways of curing an illness spiritually. One is to put a force of consciousness and truth on the physical spot which is affected. The effect produced depends naturally on the receptivity of the person, but the force of consciousness is put on the affected part, and its pressure restores order.

If the body lacks receptivity altogether, or if its receptivity is insufficient, one sees the inner correspondence with the psychological state which has brought about the illness, and acts on that. But if the cause of the illness is refractory, not much can be done. Let us say the origin is in the vital being. The vital being absolutely refuses to change; it clings to the condition in which it is. Then it is hopeless. Usually the force of consciousness then provokes the illness because of the resistance of the vital being, which did not want to accept anything. I speak of the vital being, but it could be the mind, or something else.

When the force of consciousness acts directly upon the affected part of the body, relief is possible. Then, some hours or even a few days later, the illness returns. This means that the cause has not been changed; the cause is still there in the vital being, and it is only the effect that has been changed. But if one can act simultaneously on both the cause and effect, and the cause is sufficiently receptive to change, then the person is completely cured, once and for all.

Control of blindness is now a global effort, and the International Lions Foundation has agreed to raise hundreds of millions of dollars, and they recently agreed to finance our whole institute. The American Academy of Ophthalmologists is also committed to supporting the global effort. So things do happen, slowly and steadily. There are higher forces at work in these situations, and the global solutions to blindness are beginning to take shape. In 1984, when we wanted to build another hospital one hundred miles to the south of Aravind, we were told it would cost about one million dollars. We discovered that we could raise it from our own paying patients, and so we did. I had no plans at all in the beginning for how this was going to come about, but things evolve, consciousness evolves, and that gives me moral support. Recently we expanded our old building, and all of the money has come from our own earnings from patients who can afford to pay according to their capacity. We generate money from paying patients, use it optimally, and we are able to take care of a large volume of poor patients, build good buildings and bring our services up to an international standard.

Perhaps a school of divinity is the ideal place for people to work on this higher consciousness, to challenge scientists and others to discover a higher consciousness and learn how to grow into that consciousness in daily life—not by going to a monastery, or leading a secluded life. How can we make the best use of the instruments we have, mind and body, so that the whole being is changed?

Sri Aurobindo observed:

Spirituality is not intellectual. It is a sign that a power greater than the mind is striving to emerge. Spirituality is a progressive awakening to the inner reality of our being, to a spirit, a self, a soul, which is other than mind, life, body. It represents an inner aspiration to know and to enter into contact or union with a greater reality—one which also pervades the universe and dwells within us. As a result of that aspiration, that contact, and that union, there is a conversion, a turning, a birth into new being. Only spiritual realization and experience can bring about the transformation of our mental beings into spiritual beings.

If the final goal of terrestrial evolution were only to awaken human beings to the supreme reality and release them from ignorance and bondage, so that the liberated soul could find a higher state of being or merge with this supreme reality, the task could be accomplished with the advent of a spiritual being. But there is also in us an aspiration to transform and master nature, to perfect earthly existence itself. Permanently establishing a new order of existence demands a radical change of the entire human nature. There are three phases to this transformation. First, the soul or psychic being has to come forward and lead the whole being. The spiritual change culminates in a permanent ascension from the lower consciousness to the higher consciousness, followed by an effective permanent descent of the higher nature into the lower nature. Second, a new consciousness begins to form with new forces of thought and sight, and a power to direct spiritual realization which is more than thought or sight. To make this new creation permanent and perfect, the very foundation of our ignorant nature must be transfigured; a great power, a supramental force must intervene to accomplish that transfiguration, and that is the third phase—supramental transformation.

It is difficult to conceive intellectually what the supermind is. To describe it would require a language other than our mind's poor, abstract one. But we can say that the transition from mind to supermind is a passage from nature to supernature. For that very reason, it cannot be achieved by a mere effort of our mind, or our unaided aspirations. Overmind and supermind are both involved and hidden in earthly nature; but their emergence in us requires the powers of the superconscience to descend to us, to lift us up and transform our being.

But in what way is this going to help us? There is so much misery, so much suffering. Yet if it is possible to eradicate a disease like smallpox, it is possible for the human body to improve and perfect itself, so that it can prevent diseases from overwhelming us. All modern science looks for such answers, but the scientific world has not been able to help in the way the higher consciousness can help, to bring harmony, light and truth wherever there is darkness—from disease, from drugs, from war and violence. In our work, though we are confining ourselves to the control of blindness, we are also interested in seeing how we can grow in our consciousness, and whether we can become a new human being, not with a mind groping in darkness, but a human being who is a better instrument, an improvement, just as the electron microscope is an improvement upon the ordinary microscope. For the new consciousness, the new supermind, will be able to see a thing in its truth.

It is very important for modern humanity to see just how spiritual people think and work. At the end of a long and moving passage in his diary, dated February 8, 1913, Sri Aurobindo wrote the following words. Perhaps they are the best indicator of his own spiritual powers, and of how spiritual powers and forces can work:

All depends on the spirit in which a thing is done, the principles on which it is built, and the use to which it is turned...[In the *Bhagavad Gita*] Krishna calls upon Arjuna to carry on war of the most terrible kind, and by his example encourages men to do every kind of human work. Do you contend that Krishna was an unspiritual man and that his advice to Arjuna was mistaken or wrong in principle? Krishna goes further and declares that a man—by doing in the right way and in the right spirit the work dictated to him by his fundamental nature, temperament and capacity, and according to his and its *dharma*—can move toward the Divine...It is in his view quite possible for a man to do business and make money and earn profits and yet be a spiritual man, practice yoga, have an inner life. The *Gita* is constantly justifying works as a means of spiritual salvation and enjoining a Yoga of Works as well as of *Bhakti* [Devotion] and Knowledge. Krishna, however, superimposes a higher law also that work must be done without desire, without attachment to any fruit or reward, without any egoistic attitude or motive, as an offering or sacrifice to the Divine. This is the traditional Indian attitude towards these things, that all work can be done if it is done according to the *dharma*, and if it is rightly done, it does not prevent the approach to the Divine, or access to spiritual knowledge and the spiritual life.